DELTA BLUE

(THE MADNESS)

RUSSELL G. ROBISON

Llumina Press

ISBN: 1-932560-12-2
Printed in the United States of America by Llumina Press

DEDICATION

THIS BOOK IS DEDICATED TO ALL THE MEN AND WOMEN OF THE UNITED STATES ARMED SERVICES WHO HAVE SERVED AND ARE SERVING OUR COUNTRY. WITH A VERY SPECIAL THANKS TO THE MOBILE RIVERINE FORCE, TF116, TF117, THE 9TH INFANTRY AND 3RD SURGICAL UNIT AT DONG TAM, RVN. I REMEMBER EVERYDAY...

RUSSELL ROBISON
GMG3—USN
NAVAL SUPPORT ACTIVITY
DONG TAM, RVN
FEB 68---MAY 70

FOREWORD

I WALKED AMONG GIANTS, AND THEY CALLED ME BROTHER …

RUSSELL G. ROBISON GMG-3
UNITED STATES NAVY
NSA-DONG TAM RVN
FEB 68—MAY 70

TABLE OF CONTENTS

MAY WE ALWAYS REMEMBER THOSE WHO
SURRENDERED THEIR TOMORROWS,
SO THAT WE MIGHT HAVE TODAY

DELTA BLUE

DELTA BLUE

...THE MADNESS...

DELTA BLUE

THERE CAME A TIME NOT LONG AGO.
IN A TIME NO ONE SHOULD KNOW,
WHEN DARKNESS CAME TO CLOUD THE SKY
AND LIES WERE TRUTH. YES, TRUTH DENIED.

AND ALL THE FLOWERS WE HAD BORNE
WERE LEFT ALONE TO FACE THE STORM,
WHILE THEY ALL RAN TO HIDE THEIR SHAME
AND SOUGHT US OUT TO PLACE THE BLAME.

BUT THEY KNEW NOT THE PRICES PAID.
NO, THEY KNEW NOT THE DEMONS MADE.
TOO HIGH A PRICE, NOW THIS WE KNEW.
THAT'S WHY THEY CALLED US DELTA BLUE.

DELTA BLUE

JUSTICE

HE VIEWED THE LAND WITH NAKED THOUGHT
AND SAW HIS COUNTRY AS A ROCK
THAT STOOD IMPLANTED ON A GOAL
THAT FREE MEN ONLY WERE FREE OF SOUL.
AND WITH THIS THOUGHT HE TURNED ONCE MORE
PICKED UP HIS JUSTICE AND MARCHED TO WAR.

DELTA BLUE

I REMEMBER EVERYDAY

IN THE SHADOWS OF THE DARKNESS
IN THE MADNESS OF THE FIGHT,
IT DOESN'T REALLY MATTER NOW
WHO IS WRONG OR RIGHT.

DID I SEE GOD'S FACE THAT NIGHT?
DID I FEEL HIS GRACE?
AS THOSE AROUND ME FALTERED, FELL...
IN THAT ANGRY PLACE...

OH I KNOW NOT WHY I REMAIN
WHILE AROUND ME BROTHERS DIED.
THERE'S GUILT THAT BURNS INSIDE ME,
THAT WITH THEM I DON'T ABIDE.

BUT LIFE GOES ON THEY TELL ME.
THEY'RE GONE, SO LET IT LAY.
BUT THEIR FACES, NAMES, AND COURAGE
I REMEMBER EVERY DAY...

DELTA BLUE

WARRIOR

HE WAS A WARRIOR
AND HIS HEART WAS TRUE.
YES HE WAS A WARRIOR
WHAT ELSE COULD HE DO?

SOMEONE MUST FIGHT NOW
YES SOMEONE MUST TRY,
BUT IT WAS INSANE NOW
THAT SO MANY MUST DIE.

HE SUFFERED IN SILENCE
NIGHTS SHATTERED BY SCREAMS,
IGNORED BY HIS COUNTRY
WITH HIS SCARS SO EXTREME.

BUT HE WAS A WARRIOR
AND HIS HEART WAS TRUE.
YES, HE WAS A WARRIOR
WHAT ELSE COULD HE DO?

DELTA BLUE

VETERANS DAY

(For Toby Davies Radioman USN)

WE STOOD THERE IN THE SILENCE
THAT ONLY COMES WITH TEARS
WE KNELT BESIDE A BROTHER LOST
WHO NO LONGER SHARED OUR FEARS.

WE WEPT AGAIN THAT MORNING
FOR A BROTHER GONE AWAY
THERE WAS ONLY FIGHTING LEFT FOR US
WHAT MORE WAS THERE TO SAY?

BUT AS WE TURNED TO LEAVE HIM
WE PRAYED GOD FOUND HIM FAIR
FOR ONLY GOD COULD KNOW THE PRICE
WE PAID TO LEAVE HIM THERE...

DELTA BLUE

TIME

THE CYCLE, THE CIRCLE, SHE ALWAYS RUNS TRUE
NO MATTER THE PROBLEMS THAT MAN MIGHT CONSTRUE.
UNHEEDED, SHE DEFTLY DISPOSES OF DREAMS
BEARS WITNESS IN SILENCE TO ALL OF OUR SCHEMES.

AND JUST LIKE A RIVER WHOSE CURRENT RUNS DEEP,
SHE FLOWS ON FOREVER NEVER PAUSING TO SLEEP.
TO HER WE ARE FLEETING SO BRIEF IS OUR FLIGHT
FOR WE ARE BUT MOMENTS THAT OCCUR IN HER SIGHT.

SHE'S THE ENDING, BEGINNING, EACH MOMENT REBORN
SHE'S THE SUNRISE, THE SUNSET...ETERNAL IN FORM.
SHE'S THE CYCLE, THE CIRCLE, SHE ALWAYS RUNS TRUE.
BETTER DO UNTO HER ' FORE SHE DOES UNTO YOU.

DON'T YOU KNOW TIME'S ENDLESS HIGHWAY
JUST KEEPS ROLLING ON AND ON.
BETTER GET ON BOARD AND RIDE MY FRIEND
BEFORE YOUR TIME IS GONE.

DELTA BLUE

FATE IS THE HUNTER

FATE IS THE HUNTER.
DEATH IS THE PRIZE.
GOD'S THE CREATOR.
BUT EVERYTHING DIES.

AND IN OUR PASSING
ARE WE REBORN?
OR IS IT THAT MAN
IS THE ULTIMATE FORM?

PEACE IS A PROCESS?
WAR IS A PLAN?
BOTH ARE OUR NATURE?
I DON'T UNDERSTAND.

WE ARE HIS CHILDREN.
FORGETFUL AT BEST.
WON'T SOME GENERATION
EVER PASS HIS GREAT TEST?

THAT LOVE IS THE ANSWER
AND HATE IS THE LIE.
THERE CAN BE NO SALVATION
WATCHING HIS CHILDREN DIE.

SOME SAY I'M A DREAMER
AND OTHERS A FOOL,
BUT I'VE SEEN THE MADNESS
OF MAN WHEN HE RULES.

SO CAST OUT THAT DEMON
THAT HATE DOES ABIDE.
AND KNOW NOW THE WONDER
OF HIS LOVE DEEP INSIDE.

DELTA BLUE

THE VILLAGE

WE TURNED OUR BOAT AWAY
FROM THE VILLAGE THAT NIGHT.
IN THE DARKNESS OF THE RIVER
OUR EYE'S MET IN SILENCE,
AND SAID NO MORE...
NO MORE THIS DAY...
WE LEFT THEM IN PEACE THAT NIGHT...
WE PRAYED THEY FELT OUR LOVE,
AND FORGAVE US OUR ANGER.

DELTA BLUE

15

COME ON HOME

HAVE YOU EVER LOOKED UPON YOUR HANDS
AND SEEN THE BLOOD OF MAN?
DID YOU LOOK INSIDE YOUR SOUL
AND TRY TO UNDERSTAND?
DO YOU CRY OUT IN THE NIGHT
CALLING OUT FOR LOVE?
OR GET DOWN ON YOUR KNEES
TO SOME GOD ABOVE?

I KNOW THERE'S AN ANSWER
LYING SOMEWHERE.
I KNOW THERE'S A PATH TO LEAD ME
FROM THIS DARK DESPAIR.
FOLLOW ME BROTHER, FOLLOW ME BROTHER
COME ON HOME.

OH, I'VE BEEN KICKED WHEN I WAS DOWN LORD.
NEVER GONNA UNDERSTAND WHY,
BUT TO SOME I'M JUST A CLOWN,
A WANDERING FOOL JUST TRYING TO GET BY.
BUT ALL THOSE WHO WANDER,
BABY, ARE NOT LOST.
SOMETIMES THE PRICE GETS PAID
NO MATTER WHAT THE COST.

EVERYWHERE I GO
DARKNESS FOLLOWS ME.
SEARCHING, I WILL FIND
A WAY TO BE FREE.
FOLLOW ME BROTHER,
FOLLOW ME BROTHER,
COME ON HOME.

LONESOME HIGHWAY, YOU SOLITARY FOE.
SOMETIMES, I WONDER WHY?
I KEEP ON SEARCHING FOR THE DAWN
THAT WILL SOMEDAY LIGHT MY SKY.

BEHIND ARE ROADS OF SORROW
AS I STUMBLED THRU THE NIGHT
SEARCHING FOR TOMORROW
AND SURVIVAL IN THE FIGHT.

NOW I SEE THE ANSWER.
COME TAKE MY HAND.
THE JOURNEYS OVER
AND I UNDERSTAND.
FOLLOW ME BROTHER,
FOLLOW ME BROTHER,
COME ON HOME...

DELTA BLUE

THE SMILING FACE

THE SMILING FACE HAS LOST ITS PLACE,
BEEN SWALLOWED BY THE NIGHT,
AND THOUGH THE DAWN HAS COME AND GONE
ONLY DARKNESS FOLLOWS LIGHT.

WASTING TIME, THOUGH NOT A CRIME
SEEMS SENSELESS TO MY MIND.
BUT DIFFERENT WAYS TO DIFFERENT DAYS
CAN BE SO VERY HARD TO FIND.

ALL MY LIFE I'VE SEEN SORROW,
ALL MY LIFE I'VE SEEN PAIN.
WHEN WILL I FIND TOMORROW?
NEED THE SUNSHINE, NOT THE RAIN.

NOW I'VE BEEN TOLD BY WISE MEN OLD
THAT PATIENCE IS THE KEY,
BUT I MUST GO, FOR I MUST KNOW
NO MORE SHADOWS HAUNTING ME.

NOW COULD IT BE THAT WHAT I SEE
IS NOT JUST THRU MY EYES?
FOR THOSE OF YOU WHO KNOW IT'S TRUE
AND FINALLY REALIZE

DO NOT FEAR TO LOSE THE BATTLE,
DO NOT FAIL TO GIVE YOUR ALL.
IN THE STRUGGLE LIES THE ANSWER
REGARDLESS HOW IT FALLS.

JUST LIKE STEEL THAT'S BEING TEMPERED
BY THE WATER AND THE FLAME
YOU TOO ARE SHAPED AND HARDENED
BY YOUR STRUGGLE JUST THE SAME

DO NOT LET THY BANNER FALTER,
DO NOT WEAKEN IN THY QUEST,
DO NOT LET THE TIDE OF BATTLE
EVER STAY YOU FROM THE TEST.

AND HE WILL SHINE WITHIN YOU
AND ONE TRUTH WILL ALWAYS SHOW.
WE KEPT THE FAITH MY BROTHER
AND THAT'S ALL WE NEED TO KNOW.

DELTA BLUE

VIETNAM

WHEN I BEGAN TO KILL MY BROTHER
CAME AN EMPTINESS TO MY SOUL
AND WITH IT CAME A COLDNESS
THAT MY HEART COULD NOT CONTROL

WITH THEIR TRUMPETS IN THE DISTANCE
CAN YOU HEAR THAT AWFUL SOUND
DID YOU SEE THE SADDEST VISION
OF YOUR BROTHER ON THE GROUND

DO YOU STAND AND KEEP ON FIGHTING
WHEN YOU KNOW THE BATTLE'S LOST.
DO YOU DARE TO LOOK INSIDE YOUR HEART
AND SEE THE AWFUL COST.

IT BECAME MUCH MORE THAN KILLING
WENT BEYOND BOTH DEATH AND STRIFE.
IT ROBBED US OF OUR INNOCENSE
FROM TOO MANY IT TOOK LIFE

THERE ARE TIMES NOW, WHEN THE SUN
WILL SET AND NEVER RISE
AND TIMES WHEN YOU'RE THE ONLY ONE
TO KNOW WHAT THAT IMPLIES

DELTA BLUE

IN MEMORIAM

(For Sgt. Tony Hunt 11th Armored Cavalry Regiment)

CAN YOU TELL ME NOW MY FRIEND
WHY THE HARD TIMES NEVER SEEM TO END?
ANOTHER SOLDIER OF THE GOOD FIGHT'S ON THE GROUND
FALLEN DOWN, FALLEN DOWN, FALLEN DOWN.

SEE MY BROTHER, SEE MY FRIEND,
HIS STEP HAS FALTERED AT JOURNEY'S END.
NO MORE LAUGHTER, NO MORE RHYME
CRAZY TIME, CRAZY TIME, CRAZY TIME

BUT STILL I WONDER, WHY IT MUST BE
HE LEAVES THE BLIND BEHIND
AND TAKES THE ONES WHO SEE.
HEY MR. LANDLORD UP ABOVE, I DISAGREE
TELL ME WHY, TELL ME WHY, TELL ME WHY

WHY MUST THE GOOD ONES FALL FAST AND QUICK,
WHILE ALL THE REST OF US MANAGE TO STICK.
GOOD BYE MY BROTHER, GOODBYE MY FRIEND
NEVER DREAMED I WOULD SPEAK IN MEMORIAM.

IN MEMORIAM, I SING YOUR SONG.
IN MEMORIAM, I SING IT STRONG.
IN MEMORIAM I LIFT MY VOICE ON HIGH.
IN GOODBYE, IN GOODBYE, IN GOODBYE.

DELTA BLUE

EARTHLY HELL

OFT TIMES IT IS I GAZE ABOUT
THIS CELL THAT IS MY HOME
AND FEEL THE URGE TO SCREAM AND SHOUT
FOR I AM SO ALONE.

IT MATTERS NOT THAT ALL AROUND
OTHER VICTIMS DWELL.
THEY TOO ARE PART OF THIS MISERY
HERE IN THIS EARTHLY HELL.

EACH DAY, I AM DRIVEN FROM MY CELL
TO LABOR FOR THE STATE.
THE PAIN AND HURT ALL SEEM TO SWELL
FROM MY BITTERNESS AND HATE.
I BROKE THE LAW AND I'M DOING TIME
'CAUSE THE MAN SAYS I MUST PAY
IN THIS NIGHTMARE WHERE I FIND MYSELF
LIVING DAY BY DAY.

THUS IT IS I STARE WITHIN
TO WHERE LIES WHAT CAN'T BE CHANGED,
AND TO SOME DEGREE, I STILL AM FREE
NO MATTER HOW I'VE AGED.
UNLESS MY FRIEND YOU SHARE THIS WORLD
THERE ARE THINGS SO HARD TO TELL
BEEN HOLDING ON SO VERY LONG
HERE IN THIS EARTHLY HELL.

DELTA BLUE

TIME AND A WAY

THERE COMES A TIME.
THERE WILL COME A DAY.
GONNA FIND MY ANSWERS
OH MAYBE TODAY.
AIN'T GONNA WONDER
JUST WHERE I'M BOUND,
JUST HOPE TOMORROW'S
STILL HANGING AROUND.

WHEN I WAS A YOUNG BOY
OH MY FATHER HE SAID,
THERE WILL BE SOME TIMES BOY
WHEN YOU WISH YOU WERE DEAD.
BUT YOU BE STRONG NOW
AND YOU WILL MAKE IT I KNOW.
DON'T BE AFRAID SON,
INTO A MAN YOU WILL GROW.

NOW I'VE SEEN IT HARD,
AND I'VE SEEN IT COLD.
GET SO TIRED OF FIGHTING MY WAY
EVERYDAY.
SO I KEEP ON KEEPING ON
WITH GOD'S LOVE I'M GONNA STAY STRONG.
HOW MANY DUES ARE
LEFT FOR ME TO PAY?

THERE WILL COME A TIME.
THERE WILL COME A DAY.
GONNA FIND MY ANSWERS
OH MAYBE TODAY.
AIN'T GONNA WONDER
JUST WHERE I'M BOUND.
JUST HOPE TOMORROW
IS STILL HANGING AROUND.

DELTA BLUE

ENOUGH SAID

LONG AGO AND FAR AWAY,
WHEN SADNESS CAME TO RULE THE DAY,
WHEN RIGHT WAS WRONG, AND WRONG WAS REAL,
I NEVER LEARNED HOW NOT TO FEEL.
THOUGH THERE MY TRUTH WAS LAID TO REST,
I NEVER KNEW IT WAS A TEST.
SO THERE I STOOD IN SILENT DUES,
BEFORE THE THINGS THAT MAN CONSTRUES.
MAY GOD FORGIVE US ALL, I SAID,
AS I STOOD THERE AMONG THE DEAD.

DELTA BLUE

REGRETTABLE FLAW

TORN AND TATTERED, HER DREAMS SHATTERED
A WOMAN, SO POSSESSED BY STRIFE
SHE HAD NO HOPE, AND SHE COULDN'T COPE
WITH THE COMPLEXITIES OF LIFE

ALONE AND LOST, SHE PAYS THE COST
IN THE GRIEF THAT SHE MUST BEAR
A WOMAN POSSESSED, BY EMPTINESS
'CAUSE SHE HAD NO ONE TO SHARE

SHE LIVES IN PAIN, WITH NOTHING TO GAIN
DOOMED TO FOREVER BE
A VICTIM AFRAID, THAT SOCIETY MADE
CONSUMED BY HER MISERY

A WOMAN DENIED, EVEN HER PRIDE
FOR SOCIETY MAKES NO EXCEPTIONS
FORCED TO FACE, HER OWN DISGRACE
BY THE LAWS OWN FOUL DECEPTION

SHE COULDN'T DENY, HER CALLING TO DIE
PUTTING AN END TO HER STRIFE
BRINGING AN END, TO WHAT HAD BEEN
THE AGONY OF HER LIFE

PEOPLE WILL SAY, OF HER SOMEDAY
OH SHE SUFFERED INSANITY
A REGRETTABLE FLAW, FOUND IN THE LAW
OH THAT GOVERNS HUMANITY

DELTA BLUE

BIG MAN

BIG MAN WALKING
DOWN THE SIDE OF THE ROAD.
DON'T MESS WITH THE BIG MAN.
THAT'S WHAT I'VE BEEN TOLD.
NEVER THINKS TWICE
ABOUT THE DUES HE HAS TO PAY.
HE WALKS HIS OWN PATH.
YOU KNOW HE LIKES IT THAT WAY.

KEEP ON WALKING BIG MAN,
YOUR ROAD IS ALL CLEAR.
RELIEVE YOUR PAIN WITH WHISKEY.
YOU'LL FIND NO TROUBLE HERE.
KEEP ON TALKING BIG MAN,
WE HEAR WHAT YOU SAY.
NOW WE KNOW WE CAN DEPEND ON YOU
TO KEEP THE WORLD AT BAY

OLD MAN SITTING
IN A BEAT UP OLD CHAIR
SEES THE BIG MAN WALKING
AND HE WONDERS WHERE.
ONCE HE WAS YOUNG,
HE KNOWS THE REASON WHY
BIG MAN'S WALKING.
LET HIM WALK ON BY.

KEEP ON WALKING BIG MAN,
YOUR ROAD IS ALL CLEAR.
RELIEVE YOUR PAIN WITH WHISKEY.
YOU'LL FIND NO TROUBLE HERE.
KEEP ON TALKING BIG MAN,
WE HEAR WHAT YOU SAY.
NOW WE KNOW WE CAN DEPEND ON YOU
TO KEEP THE WORLD AT BAY

DELTA BLUE

DEAR JOHN

THERE WAS A TIME, WHEN LIFE WAS FINE
HAD MY WOMAN BY MY SIDE
BUT SHE WALKED AWAY, WHY I COULD NOT SAY
AND SOMETHING MAGIC IN ME DIED

I LOST THE TOUCH, I NEED SO MUCH
OH HER BODY PRESSING NEAR
OH SHE WARMED MY NIGHT, TOOK AWAY MY FRIGHT
AND EASED MY PAIN AND FEAR

NOW YOU'VE BEEN GONE, SEEMS SO VERY LONG
AND IT JUST DON'T SEEM THE SAME
THE LOVE WE KNEW, I THOUGHT WAS TRUE
TILL YOU BURNED ME IN YOUR FLAME

YOU WOULD NOT SAVE, THIS LOVE I GAVE
FOR MY HEART YOU WOULD NOT CLAIM
SO YOU LET ME FALL.CAUSE I WOULDN'T CRAWL
NO I WOULD NOT PLAY YOUR GAME

LEFT ME, LEFT ME FALLING
LEFT ME, LEFT ME CALLING
YOU JUST TURNED AND WALKED AWAY

OH YOU LEFT ME TRYING,
OH YOU LEFT ME DYING
I WILL NEVER FORGET THAT DAY

SO VERY STRANGE, HOW PEOPLE CHANGE
AS THEY JOURNEY ON THEIR WAY
AT FIRST IT SEEMED, I'D FOUND MY DREAM
BUT THERE WAS NOTHING LEFT TO SAY
YOU HATED ME CAUSE I WAS FREE

AND YOU WERE CHAINED BY TIME
I SAW YOUR SOUL, IT WAS BLACK AND COLD
WHO KNEW YOU WERE THE CRIME

LEFT ME, LEFT ME FALLING
LEFT ME, LEFT ME CALLING
WHEN YOU TURNED AND WALKED AWAY

OH YOU LEFT ME TRYING
YES YOU LEFT ME DYING
AND I WILL NEVER FORGET THAT DAY

DELTA BLUE

TOUCH ME

IT'S QUIET NOW, THE NIGHT IS CALM
BUT TROUBLED IS MY HEART.
NOT LONG AGO, MY LOVE SAID TO ME
COME MORNING SHE'D DEPART.

HOW DOES ONE TELL ANOTHER
OF THE PAIN INSIDE THEIR SOUL,
EXPRESS THEIR LOVE SO DEEPLY
WITHOUT LOSING ALL CONTROL?

TOUCH ME, IF JUST TO SAY GOODBYE.
TOUCH ME, I WON'T QUESTION WHY.
MAKE LOVE TO ME BEFORE THE DAWN
CALLS OUT YOUR NAME AND YOU ARE GONE.

YOU CAME INTO MY LIFE ONE DAY
WHEN YOUR TOUCH WAS NEEDED SO.
I LOVE YOU WOMAN SO DAMN MUCH
THERE'S NO WAY YOU'LL EVER KNOW.

SOMEHOW IT DOESN'T SEEM FAIR
TO WAKE AND FIND YOU GONE.
THE LOVE WHO GAVE ME HELP TO HEAL
ALWAYS THERE TO LEAN UPON.

TOUCH ME, IF JUST TO SAY GOODBYE.
TOUCH ME, I WON'T QUESTION WHY.
MAKE LOVE TO ME BEFORE THE DAWN
CALLS OUT YOUR NAME AND YOU ARE GONE.

REMEMBER ME MY LADY,
PLEASE LINGER ON OUR THOUGHT
OUR LAUGHTER, OUR SHARING, OUR LOVE
AND ALL THE DREAMS WE SOUGHT.

WOMAN, THOUGH YOU MUST GO
TELL ME WHY YOU CAN'T SEE
YOU WERE ALL THE LOVE I EVER SOUGHT
TO LIVE INSIDE OF ME.

TOUCH ME, IF JUST TO SAY GOODBYE.
TOUCH ME, I WON'T QUESTION WHY.
MAKE LOVE TO ME BEFORE THE DAWN
CALLS OUT YOUR NAME AND YOU ARE GONE.

DELTA BLUE

HAUNTING VISION

HAUNTING VISION, NOW I KNOW
AT LAST I FINALLY SEE.
I CANNOT RUN QUITE FAR ENOUGH
FROM YOU TO BE SET FREE.
GOING DOWN THAT ROAD AGAIN
NOT TOO SURE JUST WHERE I GO
SEEMS THE YEARS HAVE COME AND GONE
STILL HAVE NOTHING LEFT TO SHOW.

OH, WHY MUST TIME LOSE ALL ITS RHYME
WHEN LONELY DAYS ABIDE?
JUST DON'T KNOW HOW FAR I MUST GO.
STILL I FIND YOU BY MY SIDE.
KNOWN THE PAIN OF BEING KICKED AGAIN
JUST TO SEE IF I WAS REAL.
BUT I'M NOT SAD FOR DREAMS I'VE NEVER HAD.
FOR IT ONLY MATTERS THAT YOU FEEL.

SEEN TOO MANY SIGHTS, SPENT TOO MANY NIGHTS
LOST, SO LOST AND ALL ALONE
WITH CRAZY DREAMS, AND NIGHTMARE SCREAMS
THE SCARS OF TIMES I'VE KNOWN.
GONNA FIND THE ANSWERS
TO MY QUESTIONS SOMEWHERE
SEE THROUGH ALL THE ILLUSION
TO THE TRUTH THAT'S REALLY THERE

HAVE YOU EVER SOUGHT THE HEAVENS'?
SIRENS CALLING FROM THE DEEP?
HAVE YOU EVER SEARCHED THE VELVET NIGHT
FOR THE SECRETS IN HER KEEP?
MANY MILES BEFORE ME, MANY MILES BEHIND
HOW MUCH FURTHER, TELL ME BROTHER CAN YOU SEE?
KNOW THE ROAD'S GONNA BE MUCH BRIGHTER
WHEN THIS HAUNTING VISION,
HAUNTING VISION SETS ME FREE...

DELTA BLUE

JUST A THOUGHT

WITH TOO LITTLE TRUTH
AND TOO MANY DOUBTS
THERE'S NOT ENOUGH REASON TO FIND OUR WAY OUT.

WITH TOO MANY QUESTIONS
AND TOO MANY LIES
THEN WE ARE THE PROBLEM AND WE REALIZE

THAT TOO MANY PROBLEMS
AND TOO LITTLE TIME
MEANS WE ARE THE RHYTHM WITHOUT ANY RHYME.

DELTA BLUE

THE DARKEST SILENCE

OH IN THE DARKEST SILENCE
PLEASE HEAR ME WHEN I SAY
THAT NO ONE KNEW THE COST OF WAR
OR THE PRICE WE'D PAY.

CAN YOU HEAR IT ALL AROUND YOU
THE RUMBLE OF THE HATE
THAT WAR BRINGS DOWN UPON YOU?
WE FOUND OUT MUCH TOO LATE.

BUT YES THERE IS AN ANSWER
TO THE DARKNESS AND THE PAIN.
LET HIS LOVE RAIN DOWN UPON YOU
AND MAKE YOU WHOLE AGAIN.

OH HEAR IT TRUE AND LIVE IT.
EMBRACE IT FULL AND SEE
THAT I AM JUST A PART OF YOU,
AND YOU A PART OF ME.

DELTA BLUE

ON MY WAY

ON MY WAY, FOUND MY DAY
COME ON ALONG AND I'LL TAKE YOU THERE.
THE PRICE IS HIGH, BUT YOU CAN MAKE IT IF YOU TRY.
OH DON'T YOU SEE, IF ONLY YOU'LL DARE.

GONNA TRY UNTIL THE DAY I DIE.
IT'S NOT TIME FOR THIS MAN TO SIT DOWN.
LEND A HAND. HEY BROTHER, MAKE A STAND.
THE TIME HAS COME TO QUIT GIVING GROUND.

I WILL BE A FLAME TONIGHT
AND THOUGH MY STAR, SHE BURNS SO BRIGHT.
'TIS JUST A MOMENT LOST IN TIME.
I WILL FLICKER AND BE LOST.
REFUGEE IN A DARK VOID TOSSED.
STILL SEEKING MOUNTAINS I CAN'T CLIMB.

IF YOU'RE STRONG COME ON ALONG,
THERE'S SO MANY THINGS TO SEE.
IF YOU CAN GIVE AND DARE TO LIVE,
YOU'VE FOUND THE ROAD TO BEING FREE.

IF YOU DON'T TRY, YOU'LL NEVER FLY.
IF YOU DON'T BELIEVE, THERE'S NOTHING TO SAY,
SO YOU TAKE CARE, I JUST WANTED TO SHARE.
THE TIME HAS COME TO BE ON MY WAY.

I WILL BE A FLAME TONIGHT
AND THOUGH MY STAR, SHE BURNS SO BRIGHT,
'TIS JUST A MOMENT LOST IN TIME.
I WILL FLICKER AND BE LOST,
REFUGEE IN A DARK VOID TOSSED,
STILL SEEKING MOUNTAINS I CAN'T CLIMB.

DELTA BLUE

FREEWAY BOUND

THE TIME HAS COME TO CUT AND RUN.
THE ROAD IS CALLING, I CAN TELL.
CAN'T YOU SEE? I MUST RUN FREE
'CAUSE I'M FREEWAY BOUND TO HELL.
THEIR CRAZY GAMES, THEY'RE STILL THE SAME,
JUST ANOTHER CAGE TO BIND MY SOUL.
GONNA CHANGE MY FATE 'FORE IT'S TOO LATE
GONNA TAKE MY DREAMS AND GO.

SO MANY TIMES I'VE LOST A DREAM
IN THIS CRAZY, CRAZY GAME
BECAUSE I LISTENED TO THEIR LIES
AND BELIEVED IN THEM AGAIN.
NOW I'M HOLDING MY OWN, AND I'VE SEEN THE LIGHT.
SOME OF YOU MAY UNDERSTAND
AROUND ME PLEASE STEP LIGHTLY
FOR I AM MUCH MORE THAN YOU PLANNED.

ALL TAKE, NO GIVE, JUST LIKE A SIEVE
THEY'RE TRYING TO SUCK THE LIFE OUT OF ME
THINKING I'D TAKE AND LIVE A MISTAKE,
AND ONLY DREAM OF BEING FREE.
SO MANY YEARS ARE LOST, THAT IS CLEAR.
TO STAY IS TO DIE, SO BROTHER FAREWELL.
COME ON IF YOU CAN, AND IF YOU UNDERSTAND
'CAUSE I'M FREEWAY BOUND TO HELL.

TAKE MY HAND AND FOLLOW ME,
REACH OUT FOR YOUR STAR.
IT DOESN'T MATTER WHAT YOU HAVE,
IT MATTERS WHAT YOU ARE.
DON'T LET THEM BLIND YOU BROTHER
OR CHAIN YOU WITH THEIR LIES.
THEY'RE AFRAID OF THE DUES YOU'VE PAID.
YOU CAN SEE IT IN THEIR EYES.

DELTA BLUE

THE PAIN

IF PAIN IS ALL THAT I WILL KNOW
I PRAY THAT LIFE WILL QUICKLY GO.
I GROW SO WEARY OF THEIR GAMES
THAT BURN AND PILLAGE
RAPE AND MAIM.
MY DREAMS, MY HOPES, AND TAKE MY PEACE.
I ONLY KNOW THAT THEY MUST CEASE.

DELTA BLUE

THE HEAVEN WATCHMAN

IN THE SILENCE OF YOUR HEART
NONE ARE LOVED WITHOUT A CAUSE.
DO YOU OWE YOUR PLEASURES TO ANOTHER'S PAIN?

I ABANDONED ALL MY REASON
FOR A PASSION I MISTOOK.
WHY IS LOVE SUCH A COLD AND DEADLY GAME?

I CAST MY HEART INTO THE VOID
THAT ONCE WAS FILLED WITH LOVE.
WAS MY BLOOD SHED JUST TO FUEL AN EGO'S FLAME?

WHEN THEY TRIED TO FIND MY REASON
FOR LOVING A JUST CAUSE.
MY WOUNDS PUT ALL THEIR ARGUEMENTS TO SHAME.

SO NOW I'VE CLOSED THE DOOR
TO PROTECT MY HEART
THE HEAVEN WATCHMAN GIVES ME POWER

GIVES VIRTUE TO MY SOUL
AND PROTECTS A HEART ONCE SOLD,
THE HEAVEN WATCHMAN IN MY TOWER

DELTA BLUE

MAD DOG

COLD WIND COMES BLOWING
DOWN ALLEYS DARK AND GREY.
MAD DOG, HE COMES WALKING
LOOKING FOR PREY.
IF YOU RUN YOU LOSE THE SUN.
IF YOU HIDE, YOU'LL NEVER RIDE.

WHEN MADDOG CALLS, SAINTS THEY FALL.
DEMONS FEAR WHEN MADDOG IS NEAR.

MAD DOG, HE AIN'T LOOKING FOR TROUBLE,
BUT MADDOG HE DON'T STEP ASIDE.
BROKEN BODIES ALL BEHIND HIM
OF ALL THE FOOLS WHO TRIED.
BLOCK HIS WAY AND YOU WILL PAY
SOME THAT SURVIVED AREN'T EVEN ALIVE.

WHEN MADDOG CALLS, SAINTS THEY FALL.
DEMON'S FEAR, WHEN MADDOG IS NEAR...TONITE

COLD WIND COMES BLOWING
DOWN ALLEYS DARK AND GREY.
MADDOG COMES WALKING
LOOKING FOR PREY.
IF YOU RUN, YOU LOSE THE SUN.
IF YOU HIDE, YOU'LL NEVER RIDE.

WHEN MADDOG CALLS, SAINTS THEY FALL.
DEMONS FEAR, WHEN MADDOGS NEAR.

DELTA BLUE

RUNNING SCARED

SHE CAME RUNNING THRU THE NIGHT
TRYING TO FIND HER WAY HOME.
SOMEWHERE BEHIND HER CAME HER FRIGHT
PUSHING HER EVER ON.

RUNNING SCARED
BECAUSE NO ONE CARED.
REACHING FOR THAT DOOR
NOT A HAND FOR HER NO MORE.

JUST SOME SHELTER FOR HER HEAD
MAYBE FIND ANOTHER WAY
SEEK THE ANSWER TO IT ALL INSTEAD.
THERE HAS TO BE A BRIGHTER DAY.

WITH NO MORE...
RUNNING SCARED
'CAUSE NO ONE CARED
REACHING FOR THAT DOOR
NOT A HAND FOR HER NO MORE.

SHE'S GONE NOW, RUNNING STILL
DOWN HIGHWAYS OH SO LONG.
AND I WONDER IF SHE EVER WILL
FIND A WAY TO SING HER SONG.

WITH NO MORE
RUNNING SCARED
CAUSE NO ONE CARED
REACHING FOR THAT DOOR
NOT A HAND FOR HER NO MORE.

DELTA BLUE

LOVELY LETA

LET ME TELL YOU A STORY ABOUT A WOMAN I KNOW.
THEY CALL HER LOVELY LETA AND I DO LOVE HER SO
SHE COMES BY, JUST TO SAY HI
AND TO SEE IF SHE'S STILL GOTTA HOLD.

LOOK OUT FOR YOUR HEART NOW—
HERE SHE COMES AGAIN.

SHE'S THE KIND OF WOMAN
THAT A MAN DON'T FORGET
BUT THE PRICE YOU PAY IF SHE LETS YOU PLAY
YOU'RE GONNA PAY IN SWEAT.
DON'T LOOK NOW. SHE'S GONNA HURT YOU SOMEHOW,
BUT YOU'LL NEVER REGRET
THE WAY SHE PLAYS. JUST WISHED SHE'D STAY THE NIGHT
ALL RIGHT.

LOVELY LETA, OH A BITCH IN THE GAME
CALL ME A FOOL, MAYBE I'M JUST A TOOL,
BUT I LOVE HER JUST THE SAME.
USE A MAN ANYWAY THAT SHE CAN
BUT THAT'S JUST PART OF HER GAME.

OH LOOK OUT FOR YOUR HEART NOW,
HERE SHE COMES AGAIN.

MEAN LEGGED MOMMA
OH HEAR WHAT I SAY
YOU BUILT A FIRE OF BURNING DESIRE
AND THEN YOU WALKED AWAY.
I'M STILL THE SAME, LORD I DON'T PLAY NO GAMES.
IF YOU COME BACK, COME BACK TO STAY
I GOT A NEED. AIN'T GOING TO PLEAD TONIGHT...
ALL RIGHT.

LOVELY LETA, OH A BITCH IN THE GAME.
CALL ME A FOOL, MAYBE I'M JUST A TOOL,
BUT I LOVE HER JUST THE SAME.
USE A MAN ANYWAY THAT SHE CAN
BUT THAT'S JUST PART OF HER GAME.

OH LOOK OUT FOR YOUR HEART NOW,
HERE SHE COMES AGAIN.

**DELTA BLUE
(A TENDER LOVE BALLAD)**

FOOLISH DREAMER

WALKING DOWN THE STREET
JUST LOOKING FOR TROUBLE.
FOOLISH DREAMER,
GONNA BUST YOUR BUBBLE.

I DON'T CARE WHAT
YOU THINK IS RIGHT!
DIFFERENT KIND OF LAW
ON THE STREETS AT NIGHT.
MOVING AS FAST AS YOU CAN
TRYING TO FEEL IT ALL
THE STRONG SURVIVE
THE WEAK, THEY FALL.

DOES IT REALLY MATTER ANYMORE
IF I SHOULD CALL YOUR NAME?
YOU'RE ALWAYS OFF PLAYIN' GIMME MORE.
AND LOOKING FOR SOMEONE ELSE TO BLAME.

I SEE YOU DRIVING
IN YOUR FANCY CAR,
BUT YOU'RE NOT EVEN SURE
JUST WHO YOU ARE.

ALL YOUR MONEY
CAN'T TEACH YOU TO FEEL.
LOST ALL THE MEANINGS
IN LIFE THAT ARE REAL.

RUNNIN' ROUND, BUT YOU NEVER SEE
THINK EVERYBODY'S GOTTA FEE
I HAD TO BE STRONG
I HAD TO MOVE ON.

OH, YOU'VE FALLEN DOWN SO MANY TIMES
CAUSE YOU NEVER REALLY TRIED.
THIS OLD WORLD JUST GOES ROARING BY
WHILE YOU STAND WAITING FOR A RIDE.

FOOLISH DREAMER, HOW I LOVED YOU.
MAGIC LADY, HOW WE PLAYED.
SUCH A FIRE, SEEMED WE NEVER TIRED,
AND WHAT DREAMS WE COULD HAVE MADE.

**DELTA BLUE...ROBBIE
(A TENDER LOVE BALLAD)**

OH MY LOVE

OH MY LOVE, TELL ME WHY DO YOU WANDER
WHY MUST YOU ALWAYS, ALWAYS ROAM?
OH MY LOVE, THRU STORM AND THUNDER
WHY CAN'T YOU FIND YOUR WAY HOME?

IT'S SUCH A SHAME TO PLAY A GAME
WHERE ONLY PAIN IS YOUR REWARD.
YOU LET ME TRY TO LOVE A LIE
AT A PRICE I CAN'T AFFORD.

DID YOU NOTICE THAT THE LAUGHTER DIED
WHEN MY LOVE YOU THREW AWAY?
NOW I DON'T CARE JUST WHERE YOU WANDER.
OH MY LOVE, GONNA BE ON MY WAY...PLEASE TELL ME

WHY MUST WE STUMBLE, BEFORE WE LEARN
THAT LIFE CAN BE SO HARD TO EACH OF US IN TURN?
DO YOU KNOW THE WAY TO FREEDOM FRIEND?
HAS ANOTHER SHOWN YOU LIGHT?
CAN YOU LEAD ME FROM THIS DARKNESS
FOR I HAVE LOST MY SIGHT...LOST MY SIGHT

I'VE BEEN USED. MY HEART'S BEEN ABUSED,
MY SOUL FILLED WITH SUCH PAIN,
BUT WHAT ELSE CAN I DO MY LOVE? WHERE ARE YOU?
ONLY LOVE CAN HEAL ME AGAIN.

I'M HERE TO SAY, SOMETIMES IT JUST DON'T PAY
TO GIVE YOUR HEART, TO SOMEONE NEW.
THEY'LL TAKE YOUR HEART, AND TEAR IT ALL APART,
AND TRY TO WALK ALL OVER YOU.

I REMEMBER TOUCHING YOU WOMAN,
THE SMELL OF YOUR HAIR
AND I REMEMBER THE NIGHT I FELL
AND YOU WEREN'T THERE.
DON'T YOU KNOW THE FIRE, IT CAME AGAIN THAT NIGHT,
AND ONCE MORE I JOURNEYED, ONCE MORE TO FIGHT.

NEEDED YOUR MAGIC. I WAS LOST AND SO AFRAID.
COULDN'T FIND SHELTER FROM THE DEMONS I HAD MADE.
A MOMENT LOST AND THEN REBORN
A FIRE RENEWED BY A SPARK.
I SEEK THE FLAMING HEAVENS
FOR I CANNOT BEAR THE DARK.

THERE MUST BE ANOTHER TIME, ANOTHER ANSWER
THERE MUST BE, OH ANOTHER WAY.
OH MY LOVE, YOU WERE THE DANCER
IN ANOTHER DREAM THAT WALKED AWAY.

THE PAIN OF LOVE, OH A KNIFE THATS TURNING
IN MY HEART, YOU WERE THE ONE.
OH MY LOVE, THE FIRE IT STILL LIES BURNING
AND WE LEFT SO MUCH UNDONE.

DELTA BLUE

LOST IN ILLUSION

CALL ME A WISE MAN, CALL ME A FOOL,
BUT DON'T LEAVE IT LEFT UNSAID.
YOU MIGHT FEAR THE ANSWER, SO BE SURE IN YOUR
HEART
DON'T LET SILENCE REIGN INSTEAD.

NO MATTER THE ROAD YOU WALK, OR THE TROUBLES
YOU'VE SEEN
THAT HAVE BROUGHT YOU HERE TODAY,
IF SOMEONE HAS WRONGED YOU, SPEAK OUT YOUR HEART
FOR IN SILENCE, NOTHING WILL CHANGE YOUR WAY.

SO MANY PEOPLE GOING THEIR WAY
NOT REALLY SEEING, GOT NOTHING TO SAY.
IN SUCH A HURRY, THEY FORGET TO FEEL
LOST IN ILLUSION, WHERE NOTHING IS REAL.

LET ME TELL YOU PEOPLE, LIFE IS MEANT TO LIVE.
NEVER TRY TO TAKE FROM IT MORE THAN YOU CAN GIVE.
DON'T LET TOO MANY SORROWS FROM THE PAST
NOW TAG ALONG,
FOR THERE IS NO TOMORROW,
IF YOU STILL FEAR THE DAWN.

DELTA BLUE

WIND OF LOVE

THE WIND OF LOVE BLEW MY WAY
BUT ONLY JUST A GUST
OH WE HAD THE MAGIC
BUT NOT ENOUGH TRUST.
SO NOW I'M MOVING ON
THE SUN IS CLEAR AND SHINING BRIGHT,
BUT IT'S BEEN SO MANY, MANY YEARS
SINCE I'VE SEEN HER LIGHT.

YOU SEE TOMORROW
IT'S   ANOTHER DAY
WIND OF LOVE, BLOW MY WAY
WIND OF LOVE, BLOW MY WAY

SHE WAS JUST A SUMMER BREEZE
BUT SHE MEANT SO MUCH TO ME
IT REALLY HURT TO SEE HER GO
BUT SHE WANTED TO BE FREE.
SHE WAS SO FINE
I LOVED AND LOST CONTROL.
OH HOW SHE EASED MY MIND
IN HER MAGIC WORLD YOU KNOW.

YOU SEE TOMORROW
IT'S ANOTHER DAY.
WIND OF LOVE, BLOW MY WAY
WIND OF LOVE, BLOW MY WAY

MOVING DOWN THAT ROAD AGAIN
WITH NO PLACE I CALL HOME,
JUST A DRIFTING SPIRIT NOW
ALWAYS BORN TO ROAM.
ALL ACROSS THIS LAND I GO
UNTIL I FINALLY SEE
AT LAST ANOTHER WIND OF LOVE
COMING AFTER ME

I AM A SEEKER OF THE FLAME
I WILL RUN, I WILL RUN TILL I FALL,
AND THOUGH MY ARMS GROW WEARY
FROM TOO MANY DAYS THE SAME
I CAN STILL HEAR MY DREAMS CALL
WIND OF LOVE.

DELTA BLUE

PRAYER

I FOUND YOU IN THE DARKNESS
I FOUND YOU IN THE PAIN
I FOUND YOU IN THE MADNESS
THAT ALWAYS COMES AGAIN.

I FOUND YOU IN THE SILENCE
IN THE LAND WHERE DEMONS GROW,
YOU WERE THE SHINING BEACON
AND THE LIGHT I DID NOT KNOW.

YOU SHINED UPON MY SHADOWS
DROVE THE DARKNESS FROM MY DAY,
YOU SAID I WAS FORGIVEN
THAT YOU HAD HEARD ME PRAY.

BUT IF YOU LOOK INSIDE ME
A TRUTH I KNOW YOU'LL SEE,
THAT UNTIL I CAN FORGIVE MYSELF
I WILL WANDER NEVER FREE

DELTA BLUE

FLOWERS

I SEND TO YOU SOME VERSES
WITH A FLOWER AS THE THEME.
COULD THIS REFLECT YOUR NATURE
OR YOUR GENTLE SOFT-LIT GLEAM?
A FLOWER BEARS SO MANY JOYS,
THE GLIMPSE OF LIFE AS IT SPRINGS NEW.
NO MATTER WHAT THE FLOWER'S SIZE
ITS COLORS ALL ARE TRUE

THE WIND KNOWS WELL THE VALUE
OF THEIR TEEMING, GROWING LIFE
FOR THE FLOWER THREATENS NOTHING
BEGETS NO PAIN, INSTILLS NO STRIFE.
SUCH A SIMPLE THING A FLOWER
AT LEAST WE FIND IT SO.
WE FORGET ITS WONDROUS WORKINGS,
HAVE NO TIME TO WATCH IT GROW

SO MANY DIFFERENT FLOWERS GROW
UPON THE LAND AROUND
REGARDLESS OF THE PLACE OR CLIME
SOMEHOW THEY STILL ABOUND.
IT'S AS IF BY THEIR DECISION
THEY WOULD MAKE OUR WORLD SO BRIGHT
AND REFUSING US OUR ASPHALT LAND
BRING SOMETHING GENTLE TO OUR SIGHT

THERE'S A THING ABOUT A WAVING PLAIN
OF FLOWERS GROWING WILD
THAT STIRS THIS HEART AND SOUL OF MINE
LIKE A PORTRAIT GOD HAS STYLED.
A GENTLE PETAL WEAVING SLOW
CARESSING NOW THE WIND
IN AN ENDLESS DANCE OF SPREADING SEED
THAT TIME HAS SEEN NO END.

WHILE RAINDROPS SEEK THE FAMISHED EARTH
AND ROOTS SOON QUENCH THEIR NEED
SOON POLLEN DRAWS THE SEARCHING BEE
TO FULFILL THE MATING PLEAD.
OF FLOWERS I KNOW LITTLE
BUT BY THEIR BEAUTY I'VE BEEN MOVED,
AND THEY CONTINUE ON TODAY,
TRULY NOW THEIR POINT IS PROVED.

YOU CAN BE STRONG AND GENTLE
AND SURVIVE THRU TIME IN PEACE.
AND IF MAN WOULD SIMPLY LEARN THEIR WAY
THAT DAY ALL WARS WOULD CEASE.
OH PITY NOW, ALL MANKIND
THAT HE LEARNS NOT THEIR WAY
JUST LEARN THE ANSWER TO THEIR LIFE
OF LIVING DAY BY DAY.

COULD THIS BE THE FLOWERS' PURPOSE
TO BRING SANITY BACK TO MAN,
AND BY THEIR SILENCE AND THEIR BEAUTY
MAKE US FINALLY UNDERSTAND.

DELTA BLUE

SICKNESS

DEEP WITHIN THE SOUL OF MAN
LIES A SICKNESS UNDISTURBED.
IT'S BEEN WITH US SINCE TIME BEGAN
AND ITS HUNGER CAN'T BE CURBED.
ITS SOUL IS VISCIOUS, CRUEL AND MEAN
ITS COFFERS FILLED WITH PAIN
UNSEEN BY ALL, THIS EVIL GREW.
NOW MUCH LAND WITH BLOOD IS STAINED.

IT IS FOUND IN EVERYONE OF US
FROM OUR FOLLY IT FOUND LIFE.
NOW OUR HISTORY BEARS ITS SCARS WITH DEAD
FOR THIS EVIL CAUSED OUR STRIFE.
MANY FACES IT PRESENTS TO US
SOME ARE FREEDOM, LIBERTY
INJUSTICE, HUNGER, GLORY
THINGS WORTH FIGHTING FOR YOU SEE.

IT TAUNTS US ALL WITH POWER,
SHOWS US MURDER ISN'T WRONG
TILL WE KNOW THAT WAR'S THE ONLY WAY.
THERE'S NO RESPECT UNLESS YOU'RE STRONG.
SO MANY HEED ITS DEATH CRY
AS SO MANY HAVE BEFORE
AND THEY MARCH OFF PROUD AND JOYOUS
TO FIGHT ANOTHER "RIGHTEOUS WAR."

SUCH A SIMPLE LITTLE TINY WORD
WHERE'S IT FROM, AND WHAT'S IT FOR?
DO YOU REALLY THINK IT USEFUL
THIS CHERISHED THING CALLED WAR?
WATCH A WAR AND SEE THE "GLORY"
SEE YOUR COMRADES MARCH TO FAME,
BUT BE CAREFUL THAT YOU WIN IT
FOR THE LOSER GETS THE BLAME.

IT IS GLORIFIED AND HONORED
'TIS A THING WORTH DOING WELL.
HOW MANY MORE WILL HAVE TO DIE
IN ITS BURNING, SCREAMING HELL?
YES, MAN MUST TRULY LOVE IT
FOR HE ALLOWS IT TO GO ON.
BUT SOMEDAY HE WILL HAVE TO STOP
FOR ALL THE SOLDIERS WILL BE GONE.

BUT DON'T LET THAT DISTURB YOU.
THERE'RE STILL MANY LEFT TO KILL.
BRING YOUR FRIENDS AND HAVE A GOOD TIME
KILL A MAN AND HAVE A THRILL.
FEEL THE SILENCE BEFORE BATTLE
KNOWING DEATH IS STANDING NEAR.
BRING YOUR FRIENDS AND HAVE A PARTY
COUNT THEIR DEAD AND HAVE SOME BEER.
AND DON'T LET THEIR DEATHS CONCERN YOU
JUST BECAUSE YOU LOOK THE SAME.
WORK HARD AND KILL THEM ALL MY FRIEND.
DON'T FORGET TO RAPE AND MAIM.

REMEMBER NOW YOU NEED NOT FEAR
FOR GOD IS ON YOUR SIDE.
SO THERE'S NO WAY NOW YOU CAN FAIL
NOT EVEN IF YOU TRIED.
WE'VE A HERITAGE TO UPHOLD I SAY
AND DESTRUCTION IS OUR CRY.
AND SATISFACTION WE WON'T HAVE
TILL THERE'S NOTHING LEFT TO DIE.
SO BE PROUD AND GIVE YOUR BATTLECALL.
LET YOUR PEOPLE SCREAM FOR WAR.
FOR EARTH IS NOW A SLAUGHTERHOUSE.
IS THAT WHAT MAN'S HERE FOR?

PLEASE TAKE PRIDE IN ALL YOU'RE KILLING.
DO NOT SPARE YOUR FELLOW MAN.
CONTINUE DOWN YOUR "GLORY ROAD"
TILL YOU'VE STERILIZED THE LAND.
YES, DESTROY THE SOIL THAT SPAWNED YOU.
FEED THAT HUNGRY FILTHY SOUL
WITH GLORY, PRIDE, AND RIGHTEOUSNESS,
MARCH YOUR ARMIES TO THEIR GOAL.
AND THEN IT WILL BE OVER
PEACE AT LAST WILL TOUCH THE LAND.
NO MORE OF MAN'S DESTRUCTION
NOW I FIND THAT THOUGHT QUITE GRAND.

BUT DO YOU THINK SUCH THOUGHTS AS THESE?
OR DO YOU REALLY CARE?
ARE YOU TROUBLED BY SUCH SENSELESS WARS
SOWING DEATH BEYOND COMPARE?
CAN IT BE THAT NOW OUR COURSE IS SET
THAT OUR EVILNESS HAS WON?
I SIMPLY WON'T ACCEPT IT.
WE CAN CHANGE- IT CAN BE DONE!
WE MUST ROOT OUT THIS MALIGNANCY
SMASH IT DOWN TILL IT HAS DIED.
AND EVEN IF WE FAIL AT THIS
AT LEAST MAN WILL HAVE TRIED.

BUT QUICKLY NOW, OUR TIME IS SHORT
DELAY WE CAN'T ALLOW.
FOR OUR FUTURE DARKENS MORE EACH DAY,
IT MAY BE TOO LATE NOW.
IT HAS URGED US TO ATROCITIES
TO OUR EARTH AND FELLOW MAN,
AND UNLESS WE STAND AND FIGHT AS ONE
NO THING WE BUILD WILL STAND.
FOR IF LIFE IS TO CONTINUE
ON THIS PLANET WE CALL EARTH
OUR ATTITUDES AND WAYS MUST CHANGE
TO REPAY HER FOR OUR BIRTH.

IT IS NOW THAT WE MUST STRUGGLE
FOR THIS DEMON NEARS HIS GOAL.
THOUGH THE BATTLE WILL BE BITTER
WE ALL MUST PAY THE TOLL.
FOR IF WE LOSE THIS CONFLICT
THE END WILL SOON DRAW NIGH,
AND EVERYTHING THAT GOD PLACED HERE
WILL HAVE TO SAY GOODBYE.
DEEP INSIDE US LIES A SICKNESS
IT'S CALLED HATRED, ANGER, WAR.
IT'S FOUND IN EVERYONE OF US
CLINGING DEEP WITHIN OUR CORE.

AMEN

DELTA BLUE

THE ONE

OF ALL MY DREAMS AMD FANTASIES
AND THOUGHTS LOST DEEP IN TIME,
PERHAPS THE GREATEST DREAM OF ALL
WAS THAT YOU WOULD BE MINE.

THAT YOU WOULD BE MY WOMAN
AND I WOULD BE YOUR MAN,
TO LOVE THROUGH LIFE FOREVER
THAT NO TIME COULD EVER SPAN.

MY HEART WOULD OPEN ALL TO YOU
AS WE BOTH HEALED OUR SORROW,
NO SADNESS NOW WOULD MAR OUR LIFE
TWO AS ONE TO FACE TOMORROW.

AND DAYS WOULD SHINE WITH ALL THE GLOW
OF A LOVE THAT HAS NO ENDING.
AND TIME WOULD CEASE ITS ENDLESS FLOW
AS JOY WAS OURS FOR SPENDING.

AND NIGHTS WOULD BRING THE AGELESS WARMTH
OF OUR LOVE SO FREE AND CLEAR
AND JOY WOULD BE THE SIMPLE TASK
OF HOLDING YOU SO NEAR

DELTA BLUE

FROM THE HEART

A WISE MAN ONCE SAID SOFTLY
THAT HE DID NOT UNDERSTAND
WHY ANY CHILD MUST SUFFER.
THAT'S NOT WHAT GOD HAD PLANNED.

FOR IN OUR HATE AND ANGER
SO MINDLESS HERE WE STAND.
SHOULD WE NOT THEN FIND SORROW
IN WHAT MAN HAS MADE OF MAN?

OF ALL THE QUESTIONS ANSWERED
THROUGH TIME'S STILL CLOUDY VEIL,
WE KNOW HATE CAN NEVER CONQUER
AND LOVE CAN NEVER FAIL.

THE ROAD HE MARKED QUITE CLEARLY
THE ANSWERS GIVEN TRUE.
IT WAS HIS ONE COMMANDMENT NOW
FOR LOVING ME AND YOU.

LET LOVE ALONE DWELL IN YOUR HEART.
LET HATE FIND YOUR HEART TRUE.
AND RICHES BEYOND MEASURE
HE WILL PLACE INSIDE OF YOU.

AND OH A SPIRIT FLAMING,
NOW WHAT A SIGHT TO SEE.
BUT OH A SPIRIT LOVING
IS WHAT YOU WERE MEANT TO BE.

DELTA BLUE

DRIFTING

AS THE LIGHT BEGINS TO FADE NOW,
AS THE JOURNEY SLOWS TO END,
I SEE SO VERY CLEARLY NOW
ALL THOSE THAT I CALL FRIEND.
AS DREAMS NO LONGER BECKON,
AS HOPE NO LONGER FLIES,
WHILE TIME, THE FLEETING MASTER,
FORCES ALL TO REALIZE
THAT WHEN THE COMING TWILIGHT
COMES CALLING ON THAT DAY,
THERE WILL BE NO NEED FOR SADNESS
AND NO MORE DUES TO PAY.
NO MORE LABORS TO PURSUE NOW,
NO MORE BURDENS NOW TO BEAR,
NO MORE FIGHTING BACK THE MADNESS
OF A WORLD THAT DOES NOT CARE.
AS INDIFFERENCE GROWS TOO COMMON
WITH DENIAL NOW OUR CREED,
WE STILL SACRIFICE THE CHILDREN
TO THE IGNORANCE AND GREED

DELTA BLUE

NIGHTMARE

DRIFTING THROUGH AN ENDLESS SEA
OF EERIE SHADOWED NIGHT
WHERE ALL AROUND THE LAND IS STILL,
SWEPT CLEAN BY DEATH AND BLIGHT.

SUCH A PLACE I CANNOT FATHOM,
LAND OF DARKNESS, NOTHING CLEAR.
SLOWLY IN MY HEART IS BORN
A STIRRING THING CALLED FEAR.

HOW DID I FIND THIS EVIL TIME?
THIS PLACE I DID NOT SEEK?
I DID NOT CHOOSE THIS DARKENED SKY
NOR STERILE LAND SO BLEAK.

I BEGIN TO FEEL UNEASY.
BEADS OF SWEAT FORM ON MY BROW.
MUST FIND THE CAUSE OF ALL OF THIS DEATH
AND WHY I'M HERE, SOMEHOW.

SUCH STILLNESS, GOD IT FRIGHTENS ME.
WHAT COULD HAVE HAPPENED HERE?
ABSOLUTE ANNIHILATION!
WITH JUST THE WIND TO MAKE IT CLEAR.

AS THE EERIE SILENCE BREAKS AWAY
TO THE RUSHING, RISING WIND
THE CHARRED AND BLACKENED BRANCHES
NOW BREAK INSTEAD OF BEND.

'TIS A MOURNING WOEFUL CRY OF PAIN
THAT THE WIND SINGS OUT TO ME,
SINGING SORROWS FOR THE SPLENDORS LOST
A LAND OF BEAUTY NONE WILL SEE.

TEARS STREAM DOWN MY SWEATING FACE
AS I HEAR THE TEARFUL TALE
THE WIND GROWS EVER STRONGER
SCREAMING PAST ME LIKE A GALE.

THEN SUDDENLY THE WIND WAS GONE
AND SILENCE CAME ONCE MORE.
AND ALL AROUND THE LAND WAS STILL.
NO DREAMS WERE LEFT TO SOAR.

WHAT CHAOS BORN OF TIME'S DECAY
HAD BROUGHT THIS TIME OF STRIFE
THAT THREATENED TO DESTROY MY DAY
AND TAKE FROM ME MY LIFE?

SO MANY TIMES I'VE WANDERED
THROUGH THE NIGHT AND FAILED TO SEE
THE PATHS THAT LEAD TO LIGHT AND PEACE
THE ROADS THAT MAKE YOU FREE.

COULD YOU PICTURE TRUE THESE VISIONS?
CAN YOU SEE THIS THRU MY EYES?
WOULD YOU UNDERSTAND MY SHADOWS DEEP
THAT I'VE TRIED TO STERILIZE?

DELTA BLUE

JIMMY'S SONG

(For James Caldwell Sp4 23rd Infantry, Americal Div. U.S.Army)

HE LEARNED IT ALL TOO QUICKLY
HE LEARNED IT FAR TOO WELL
HE LEARNED IT MUCH TOO DEEPLY
FOR HIS WORDS TO EVER TELL.
HE SAW THE PRICE OF FREEDOM
AND THE COST TO MAKE A STAND
HE SAW TOO MANY BATTLES
THAT DIDN'T TURN OUT JUST AS PLANNED.
INSIDE AN ACHE STILL HAUNTS HIM
A LAND OF DARK AND COLD
HE NEVER THOUGHT COME TWENTY-ONE
THAT HE COULD BE SO OLD.
STILL, LESSONS LEARNED REMAIN NOW
ALONG WITH SORROWS TRUE,
BUT HE KNOWS JUST WHO HE DID IT FOR
HIS SWEET RED, WHITE, AND BLUE

DELTA BLUE

THAT NIGHT

WE HELD ON ALL THROUGH THE NIGHT
AND PRAYED THAT WE WOULD BE ALL RIGHT.
DECISIONS MADE SO FAR AWAY
HAD BROUGHT US HERE TO FACE THIS DAY.
AND THERE THE STRUGGLE GREW IN PAIN
TO REACH A FRENZY NONE SUSTAIN.
THE BATTLE RAGED OUT OF CONTROL
AND ON THAT NIGHT I LOST MY SOUL.
AS FEAR AND ANGER TURNED TO HATE
THE MADNESS STILL DID ESCALATE.
BRAVE MEN DYING ON EACH SIDE
CRIED OUT TO GOD AND NOT THEIR PRIDE.
AND I WILL ALWAYS HAVE THAT SIGHT
AS WE FOUGHT AND DIED THAT NIGHT.
I STILL HEAR MY DYING FRIENDS
TRAPPED IN THAT DREAM THAT NEVER ENDS
TOMORROW'S HOPE A DREAM ALAS
BUT THRU THAT DOOR WE ALL MUST PASS.
EACH MOMENT FOUND A LIFE ANEW
THE PATH BEHIND WE CAN'T UNDO.
THE ROAD WE WALKED THE SAME FOR ALL
WHO SAW THE NEED AND HEARD THE CALL.
WE HELD THE LINE, DON'T MISCONSTRUE.
TOO MANY YEARS STILL DELTA BLUE

DELTA BLUE